kids
Ministry
That Nourishes

kids Ministry
That Nourishes

Three Essential Nutrients of a Healthy Kids Ministry

Jana Magruder

B&H
PUBLISHING GROUP
NASHVILLE, TENNESSEE

Published by B&H Publishing Group
Nashville, Tennessee

Dewey Decimal Classification: 268.432
Subject Heading: CHURCH WORK WITH CHILDREN
\ RELIGIOUS EDUCATION OF CHILDREN \ MINISTERS
OF CHILDHOOD EDUCATION

5 6 7 8 9 10 11 • 22 21 20 19 18

Dedicated to my husband, Michael Magruder, a mighty man of integrity and strength who loves the Lord more than me—and loves me even more than our own three!

And, to our three—Morgan Grace, whose tender heart and beautiful spirit inspire me daily; Jason Reese, whose passion for God shows in everything he does; and Nicholas, whose inquisitive nature and curiosity about the Bible will keep me digging through the Scriptures and theology books the rest of my days! I love you all to the moon and back and infinity and all the things we say. Sugar and Love!

Contents

Foreword by Eric Geiger xiii

Introduction. 1

Chapter 1: Three Essential Nutrients of a Healthy
Kids Ministry. 5

KINGDOM EXPANDING

Chapter 2: Essential Nutrient #1: Kingdom Expanding. . 11

Chapter 3: Feed My Lambs: Casting a Kingdom-Minded
Vision. 15

Chapter 4: Feed Your Soul: Kingdom Expanding Sabbath
Practice 21

Chapter 5: Crickets in the Choir Room: Kingdom
Expanding Leadership 27

Chapter 6: Coffee Campaigns: Developing Kingdom-Minded Volunteers *and* Leaders 33

HEART TRANSFORMING

Chapter 7: Essential Nutrient #2: Heart Transforming . . 49

Chapter 8: Check Yes! Salvation on Paper 53

Chapter 9: Heretical Me: The Danger of Haphazard Discipleship 59

Chapter 10: The Velcro Gospel: Attachment Teaching . . . 67

Chapter 11: Behavior Modification: Quick Fix vs. God's Grace 75

CULTURE SHAPING

Chapter 12: Essential Nutrient #3: Culture Shaping 83

Chapter 13: Moonlight Towers: Illuminating Dark Spaces 87

Chapter 14: Hayrides and Hotdogs: Missional Family Ministry 97

Contents

Chapter 15: Balancing Act: Protecting and Preparing
Our Kids 105

Chapter 16: A Heart for the Nations: Bringing Up
Senders and Goers 111

Conclusion: Fan the Flame: Stay Faithful
in Your Calling 117

Notes 121

About the Author 123

Ways to Connect 125

Acknowledgments

First, I would like to thank my parents, Lee and Jo Wilson, who raised me in the Church and, without even trying, led by example through serving in preschool, youth, and recreation/camp ministry. I often say that I was an apprentice of you both—a teacher and a minister. God wove our stories together and I know it all began with you. I'm so honored and grateful to be your daughter.

Thank you to Zac and Jennie Allen for planting Austin Bible in our neighborhood all those years ago and calling out a ministry gift that I had always hidden in my heart. I'm eternally grateful for those years living as "villages" in the light of moonlight towers.

To John Murchison and Kevin Peck at the Austin Stone Community Church, you taught me servant leadership, how to Sabbath, and most importantly, how to multiply myself so that others could know the joy of serving the Church. Thank you for your wise counsel and discipleship in these areas.

My LifeWay Kids family, thank you for believing in me! I could not have written this book without your support and contribution. Thank you for loving children and families and thank you for your leadership and dedication as we serve the Church together. A special thanks to Landry Holmes, Chuck Peters, and Bill Emeott for helping speak into this book.

And to Michael Magruder—in many ways, you yourself could have written this book as we have journeyed together in ministry. Thank you for loving our family so well. You are a hero to us!

Foreword

As a *pastor* and as a *parent* of two young girls, I know a healthy children's ministry and a healthy Christian home seek heart transformation, not just behavioral modification. But I also know our proclivity to move away from the heart. I know that merely altering the behavior of a child (yes, my child) can seem attractive. I get it.

I mean, sometimes I just want my kids to behave, obey their mom, look an adult in the eye when answering a question, and be sweet to our friends. Teaching children values and virtues to pursue and emulate can be really appealing. After all, who would say they do not want their child to be caring, kind, responsible, or creative? No sane person wants to teach kids to be mean, lazy, and boring.

But as Christians, we know that it is very possible to teach children values, virtues, and behavior without pointing them to the One who will transform them. It is possible to emphasize characteristics without transforming their character through Christ. If values and virtues take center stage, the good news of Jesus doesn't. And without the good news of Jesus, we really teach another gospel—which is no gospel at all.

Without Jesus, values and virtues are not Christian at all. They are not responses to His rescue, not obedience from a heart melted by His grace. They are a list of things to achieve, rather than reminders to live in response to the grace we have received.

What makes the Christian faith distinct, what makes the Christian faith powerful, is not a bunch of virtues. It is Jesus— the Vine who gave His life to give us life. And if we offer kids virtues apart from the Vine, we enslave them with a new Law without the power to live out the virtues we have given them. If we teach for fruit apart from the Spirit, we fail to announce the good news that is the power of God for salvation.

On my worst days as a parent and as a pastor, all I really care about is behavior. On my best days, on the days I am most in awe of His grace, I care for their hearts. On those days, I still want obedience and kindness—but I want it as a result of what Christ is doing in their hearts.

I love serving the Church alongside Jana Magruder because she cares for the hearts of children and passionately leverages all her experiences, her training, and her gifting in that direction. She is giving her life to help kids' ministries be heart transforming, Kingdom expanding, and culture shaping—as opposed to merely character forming, church expanding, and shaped by the culture.

Jana writes this book from a very unique perspective, a perspective forged through multiple disciplines and experiences. She's currently a *leader* of a large team of kids' ministry leaders who serve tens of thousands of churches a year with curriculum, events, and training and thus sees with a broad lens what the Lord is doing in kids' ministry.

She's an *educator* who understands how children learn and grow and develop, having designed curriculum for school systems and museums, and now leading teams to design curriculum for churches.

She's a *kids' ministry veteran* who led a kids' ministry in a church plant and dealt with everything from kids' check-in to the dreaded texts from leaders bailing on Saturday night before Sunday morning.

And she is a *mom*. A really good mom with a few years more experience than Kaye (my wife) and I have. I know because my wife texts her parenting questions!

I trust her work will be helpful to you. Thank you for serving kids, for applying the gospel to their impressionable hearts.

Eric Geiger, Vice President, LifeWay Christian Resources, coauthor of *Simple Church* and *Designed to Lead*

Introduction

Take a minute and ask yourself, *Why did I get into Kids Ministry?*

We all have a story of *how* we began, but truly ponder the *why* for a minute. Some of us set out on a mission with a calling and a career path in mind—suitable undergrad degree, seminary credentials, a paid internship, and then boom—church staff position. However, many of us took a different path. Maybe you began as a volunteer at your church or maybe the pastor knew you had what it takes to be a leader. Whatever your *how* story is, we all have a similar *why*. We have felt the call to children's ministry at some point.

The reason I ask is because no matter how we all began, a typical common denominator is that we love children and desire them to know God. Yet the irony (generally speaking) is that on a daily, weekly, monthly basis—we rarely get to teach and disciple children. Oh we see them, we greet them, we may get a hug from a preschooler and a fist bump from a preteen—but if we are honest, our duties are consumed by administration, organization, recruitment, and training—of adults, not actual teaching of kids. I want this book to help us explore that in spite of all these duties, our hearts for children can still shine and we can truly create a *Kids Ministry That Nourishes* children of all ages (babies, preschoolers, school-age children, and preteens) as well as their parents and caregivers.

This book is based on three essentials that I hope you will adopt in your ministry. To help flesh out the concepts behind each essential, I've identified theme Scriptures that give biblical references and shared some of my own stories from ministry. You may or may not relate to the context—we all serve in different types of churches who conduct ministry with unique strategies; but, I hope you'll connect to the obvious shared experiences we have all had in the field.

Each chapter will conclude with "Food for Thought" questions that you can contemplate alone or, even better, with the people who serve with you. I highly encourage you to share this with your volunteers and leaders as a tool to help you lead them through what is most valuable in children's ministry and as a way to have everyone on the same page as you lead together.

Food for Thought Questions

1. Why did you get into Kids Ministry? Share your how and why story.
2. How much time do you spend with kids versus adults in your ministry?
3. Do you currently have a ministry that nourishes the hearts and souls of children and their families?

Chapter 1

Three Essential Nutrients of a Healthy Kids Ministry

And Jesus grew in wisdom and stature
and in favor with God and people.
—LUKE 2:52

To begin our conversation about building a *Kids Ministry That Nourishes*, I think it is important to have a look at the meaning(s) of the root word *nourish*. As you can see from the definition on page 6, the word *nourish* has synonyms that are highly relatable in ministry—especially in Kids Ministry.

We want to supply what children truly need, to cherish and foster, to strengthen and build up. All of these definitions help give depth to the subject of this book. But, the one I really want to camp out on is the first bullet—to sustain with food or in this case, with nutriment.

> ## Nourish
> - to sustain with food or nutriment
> - to supply with what is necessary for life, health, and growth
> - to cherish, foster, keep alive
> - to strengthen, build up, or promote

So, what are the three Essential Nutrients of a healthy Kids Ministry? Don't worry, this is not a book about childhood nutrition and the need to switch from gluten-laden Goldfish to Styrofoam Rice Chex for Sunday snacks! There are plenty of parents in your midst that can educate you about that decision. Nutrients are the substances that provide nourishment essential for growth and the maintenance of life. The body cannot synthesize these nutrients on its own. They must be provided by the diet and are necessary for the body to function properly.

Now, we've already established that we aren't talking about food. This is simply an analogy for how to nourish the children and families whom God has placed in your ministry. What you provide is essential to the growth (or lack of growth) spiritually in the lives and hearts of boys and girls. The Three Essential Nutrients of a healthy Kids Ministries are:

- Kingdom Expanding

- Heart Transforming

- Culture Shaping

The book is divided into three parts. Each part will have chapters that unpack the philosophy and meaning behind the Essential Nutrient plus practical stories and strategies that can help you implement immediately. My prayer is that you will be refreshed and equipped to finish the race of what God has called you to do—nourish the hearts of children.

Food for Thought Questions

1. What are some things you can identify as being "Essential Nutrients" in your ministry?

2. Using the analogy, what are some non-essentials in your ministry?

3. Just for fun—Rice Chex or Goldfish?

Part 1

Kingdom Expanding

Essential Nutrient: Healthy Kids Ministry should be Kingdom Expanding, not simply ministry building.

Chapter 2

Essential Nutrient #1: Kingdom Expanding

*"But seek first the kingdom of God
and His righteousness, and all these
things will be provided for you."*
—MATTHEW 6:33

ealthy Kids Ministries should have a Kingdom Expanding foundation and mind-set. This means that before you can even begin to recruit a volunteer base, select curriculum materials, set up classrooms, or plan any kind of programming, you have to get the ultimate goals and objectives straight for conducting a ministry that always has Kingdom expansion in mind. This is different than planning how to build up your ministry, and quite frankly it can be a fine line.

Many of us want to start with *how* we are going to conduct ministry, not the *why* behind what is driving the ministry to begin with—the gospel. For example, when I first started in ministry, my first objective was to produce the best VBS experience the church had ever known. I was going to immediately implement weekly parent communication, and I was going to amp up our large group worship experience. Looking back, I know now that I was completely focused on the ministry building aspect of my job. There was nothing wrong with the goals I set out to do; they were just mis-prioritized.

It is important to start with the end in mind. For those of us in Kids Ministry, I think we can all agree on the fact that our ultimate desire is to see children understand who Jesus is and receive Him as their Lord and Savior. We want to see them saved from their sin. We want to see families who are changed because their child has a contagious faith that brings them back to church. We all know "the scary statistic" that keeps us up at night. Many researchers have concluded that a child's spiritual identity is set by age thirteen. That is about the time they leave Kids' Ministry. And that is precisely why your ministry must be about expanding God's Kingdom— meaning, introducing kids to Jesus and discipling them.

So, this is where we must begin—with a Kingdom Expanding foundation and mind-set. The next few chapters will help clarify what this means and go more in-depth for implementation in your own ministry.

Food for Thought Questions

1. Do you ever mis-prioritize ministry building goals with a Kingdom Expanding mind-set? Name some examples.

2. What words come to mind when you read statistics about a child's spiritual identity being set by age thirteen?

3. How can you begin laying a Kingdom Expanding foundation in your ministry?

Chapter 3

Feed My Lambs: Casting a Kingdom-Minded Vision

"Come, ye children, hearken unto me—
I will teach you the fear of the Lord."
—Psalm 34:11 (KJV)

Charles Spurgeon wrote a book on children's ministry called *Come Ye Children*.

It is possibly the most helpful ministry book I have in my library because every time I felt myself slipping into a helpless funk of burnout, I would flip through the pages of this tiny little book chock-full of wisdom and truth. This nineteenth-century British pastor, hailed as the "Prince of Preachers," truly understood and championed the value and urgency of teaching children. The first chapter is titled "Feed My Lambs" and begins with these words:

> The best of the church are none too good for this work. Do not think because you have other service to do that therefore you should take no interest in this form of holy work, but kindly, according to your opportunities, stand ready to help the little ones and to cheer those whose chief calling is to attend to them. To us all this message comes: "Feed My lambs." To the minister, and to all who have any knowledge of the things of God, the commission is given. See to it that you look after the children that are in Christ Jesus.[1]

Okay, can I get an amen to that? Thank you, Pastor Charlie! I'm not sure I've ever heard any pastor quip so eloquently about the absolute necessity to pour into the discipleship of children. He understood the fact that to be a church that is Kingdom Expanding in its focus, you must start with the children. That is the mind-set that keeps not only kids' ministries healthy, but the Church overall. I encourage you to use this as a way to cast vision at the leadership table where you sit as a staff member. Your pastor and fellow colleagues in ministry need to hear this from you. Maybe even buy them a copy of *Come Ye Children* for Christmas!

The overall vision, mind-set, and philosophy of your ministry must be based on expanding God's Kingdom. Sometimes this could be confused with building up our own ministry based on the attendance and baptisms posted in the bulletin. There's nothing wrong with great record keeping—it just can't be what drives us. An authentic desire to see children be adopted as sons and daughters into the Kingdom of God is what should keep us up at night, yet awaken us early—eager to do Kingdom work.

If we are only driven by numbers, there is a chance we might be chasing attractional environments and flashy programming. In other words, not focused on the nuts and bolts of ministry but the bells and whistles. This can be exhausting and lead to burnout by the time you've had your first Xbox system installed in the lobby.

Now, don't hear me say that you should not have fun and familiar environments that help kids feel welcome and safe. If your budget allows and your church context supports the approach, go for it! And certainly don't hear me say that programming is bad—as a parent, I need my church to offer high-quality, biblical programming that my kids **want** to attend. Just don't spend all your time and energy building up *your* ministry, which could take your eye off the ultimate goal of expanding *the* Kingdom.

The biggest take-away for having a Kingdom Expanding ministry is to focus on the gospel, beginning with your own heart health and the vision you cast to those who serve alongside you. Once those things are in place, you are set up to lock arms and feed lambs.

Food for Thought Questions

1. Reread the Spurgeon quote at the beginning of chapter 3 and discuss what it means to you.

2. Discuss the difference between "bells and whistles versus nuts and bolts." How does your ministry reflect these?

3. How can you cast the vision of "feeding lambs" to your staff and even church family?

Chapter 4

Feed Your Soul: Kingdom Expanding Sabbath Practice

"Come to Me, all of you who are weary and burdened, and I will give you rest. All of you, take up My yoke and learn from Me, because I am gentle and humble in heart, and you will find rest for yourselves."
—MATTHEW 11:28–29

I f you want to have a Kids Ministry that truly nourishes, then you must nourish and feed your own soul. We have established that it is essential for a healthy children's ministry to be focused on the expansion of God's Kingdom, not merely building up individual ministry goals. In order to do that, you need to start with yourself—are you ready for this kind of ministry? Kingdom-minded people must be rested up for diligent Kingdom work, and therefore must Sabbath regularly.

I use the word *Sabbath* here as a verb, not a specific day. The truth is, most ministry leaders don't get to have a work-free, restful Sabbath on Sundays (or Saturdays, or whenever your church has a primary Bible study and worship experience). Maybe you do get to slip in the back of the worship center and hear the first half of the sermon, but more than likely, you are filling in for absent volunteers or helping a child who is screaming for Mama to return! Sundays are "go-days" for you and if you want to get through them with a joyful heart, then you must take time to Sabbath with the Lord on another day. I realize that not everyone reading this has the luxury to take a different day off in the week. Some of you are volunteer or bi-vocational and a "day off" during the week is just not in your benefit package (or lack of one). However, I challenge you to find ways to Sabbath in spite of your official schedule. Perhaps it is an evening during the week or a Saturday afternoon. Once you've carved out some time in your week, decide how you are going to spend that time. Sabbath is not only about rest (sleeping and pleasure).

Note what Priscilla Shirer says in her Bible study *Breathe: Making Room for Sabbath* on this very topic. "God always and eternally intended the Sabbath to be a lifestyle—an attitude, a perspective, an orientation for living that enables us to govern our lives and steer clear of bondage."[2]

So, what does this look like for you? It will look different for all of us. For me, I enjoy an extra cup of coffee while doing Bible study leisurely, not rushed. I also enjoy taking a walk in my neighborhood, taking a special lunch to my kids at school, writing letters of encouragement to loved ones or coworkers. I try not to get on social media, constantly check e-mail, or start a project I cannot finish. I do, however, enjoy working on my home—organizing rooms, planting flowers, or stocking the pantry with fresh food. I absolutely love making dinner when I'm rested—not as a rushed "have-to" at the end of a busy day.

Sabbath takes planning—it does not happen by accident. If you say to yourself, "I'll just play it by ear this week and see what free time comes up," it will never reveal itself to you. Satan's favorite game is to keep us busy—and those of us living the American lifestyle fall trap into this scheme all too often. Therefore, it is absolutely necessary to plan—I mean ink it on the calendar, bold it in your phone with reminders, and block the hours on anyone else's calendar who might need to know that you are not available! Spouses, friends, and family are usually very understanding of your time—if they know you are unavailable ahead of time. So, be diligent planners about your Sabbath regiment. If you aren't caring for your own heart, it gets too cluttered with the busyness of life and ministry to be Kingdom-minded. Feed your soul so that you can be ready to feed the lambs in your ministry and conduct a healthy Kids Ministry that nourishes.

Food for Thought Questions

1. Describe the difference between *Sabbath* as a noun and *Sabbath* as a verb. How do the two meanings apply to you?

2. How can you "Sabbath" by resting in the "joy of what God has done"?

3. How does your Sabbath apply to a Kingdom Expanding mind-set?

Chapter 5

Crickets in the Choir Room: Kingdom Expanding Leadership

*For you were called to be free, brothers; only
don't use this freedom as an opportunity for the
flesh, but **serve one another** through love.*
—GALATIANS 5:13, EMPHASIS ADDED

Sunday mornings for me always began at 5:30 a.m. I'd
roll out of bed, get dressed, make a quick to-go coffee,
and head out—leaving sleeping family behind. My "set-up"

team would be arriving at 7:00 a.m., but I always liked to sweep and clean up as much as possible before they got there. After all, our church met at a public middle school in our neighborhood, and while the facilities met our needs, it still didn't change the fact that thousands of middle-schoolers cycled through there everyday, and it wasn't the cleanest place to put kids (much less babies and toddlers).

Therefore, as soon as I arrived I checked the bathrooms to make sure all toilets were flushed and decent (relatively speaking) and then grabbed a broom and started sweeping—lots of dirt, the occasional roach, and a ton of dead crickets. Why dead crickets? I don't really know—some kind of insect epidemic. All I do know is that they were gross and they were everywhere, but especially in the choir room where our large group worship time was held. You know the kind of school choir room where there are tiered levels for standing in formation. However, when our kids weren't standing and singing, they were sitting—on the floor. The cricket-ridden floor.

So, I swept and swept this very large choir room every Sunday and prayed over the space as I gazed upon the rock bands Green Day and No Doubt posters (clearly this choir teacher was a '90s music fan). I was careful to keep her sheet music and notes intact on her music stand and memorize exactly where to push the piano back in place. I prayed for her too—and all the middle school students who would come through this space. It was the quiet before the "storm of Sunday morning" would joyfully begin. It was my time to serve quietly in a menial, yet necessary task, of sweeping the crickets while praying for the morning.

Afterward, it would be time to meet the set-up team, unlock our pod in the parking lot, and start rolling out the enormous carts filled with all of our Sunday supplies, hoping that no rodents had found their way to the Goldfish! Classrooms would be photographed on phones as to put back in place perfectly for the teacher whose room we rented on Sundays. Little tables and mini chairs would be brought in for the preschoolers, huge carpets and toys for the toddlers, and quilts and portable, folding rocking chairs for the babies.

The elementary kids would have plenty of crafts and games awaiting them, a class set of Bibles, and CD players with worship songs playing as they arrived. Diaper changing supplies, play pens for naps, cleaning wipes for sterilizing toys, pagers, and electronic check-in systems, the list goes on and on. All of these things were stored in dozens of boxes that were hauled in from the pod and lovingly set up every Sunday to hold church in a school. And after it was over, we tore it all down, packed it all up, and put everything back in place. Every now and then a projector screen had to be replaced if a preschooler got a hold of a marker, but for the most part—it was like we were never there.

Needless to say, it was a very labor-intensive job and sometimes I resented that. The Enemy's voice in my head would make me feel like I wasn't appreciated—*I mean does this church body even know what I have to do to host their children every week? Do my volunteers understand that I swept crickets an hour before they arrived? Does the rest of the staff know that I threw my back out lifting huge boxes out of a storage unit?* I had my little fits, but the Lord got hold of my heart and taught me that leadership is not only building teams, training volunteers, and developing content. Those are part of leadership, but so is the part that goes unseen by others. The tasks that feel like someone else should be doing them.

In his book *Spiritual Leadership*, J. Oswald Sanders describes how spiritual leadership and servant leadership go together. He states, "Those who aspire to leadership seek an honorable task. The church needs more leaders, not less, but the kind of leaders we need are "authoritative, spiritual, and sacrificial."[3] Kingdom-minded leadership involves sacrifice— even suffering at times for the sake of the gospel.

I don't know what those tasks are for you—they are different for all of us. Some of you may be in charge of sorting hundreds of craft supplies, for pouring snacks in Dixie cups, for reconfiguring shared space, or for making endless copies. For me, it was sweeping crickets and lifting boxes. But, let me challenge you as I did myself—don't grumble about these things lest you be robbed the joy of serving the youngest of these. Don't miss the delight of praying over spaces that could be the very place a child hears God's voice for the first time.

And don't miss the opportunity to lovingly care and pray for another community that meets in that room the rest of the week—such as a teacher and a slew of teenagers.

Leadership in your ministry often happens when no one is looking and this is precisely the servant leadership that must be modeled in order to implement a Kingdom Expanding ministry. It is essential. It is a nutrient that can't be fabricated and therefore you need this in the DNA of everything you do—even quietly when no one sees. Conducting a *Kids Ministry That Nourishes* means making sure even the most basic needs are met before children and their families ever enter the building.

Food for Thought Questions

1. What are some tasks you do that no one knows about?
2. How is Kingdom Expanding leadership truly servant leadership?
3. How does feeding your soul help you serve others?

Chapter 6

Coffee Campaigns: Developing Kingdom-Minded Volunteers *and* Leaders

All Scripture is inspired by God and is profitable for teaching, for rebuking, for correcting, for training in righteousness, so that the man of God may be complete, equipped for every good work.
—2 TIMOTHY 3:16–17

In order to lay the foundation of a Kingdom Expanding Kids Ministry, you need a well-cast vision, a well-fed soul, a servant leadership mind-set, and last but not least—an army of volunteers and leaders who understand the Kingdom Expanding essential and can serve alongside you. My team at LifeWay Kids and I communicate regularly with church leaders from around the country and world. The number one pain point that we hear about is the desperate need for volunteers—which I'm sure is not surprising to you!

It was my number one pain point when I was on church staff—to the point where it brought me to my knees from anguish. I was in a desperate state. See if you can relate to my story. I was on staff at a large, multi-site, mobile church. I oversaw one of our campuses—remember the one in the middle school? We had a unique demographic of young families with lots of children whom many had chosen to also foster and/or adopt in addition to having biological children. The bottom line was the kids were outnumbering the adults! I was so overwhelmed with the demands of doing mobile ministry because recruiting volunteers was more than just enlisting teachers and caregivers, but also set-up and tear-down teams.

So, I did what most any wise leader would do, I begged the pastor to make more announcements from the pulpit about needing more workers, I made fliers and posted them in the restroom stalls (that'll get 'em), and sometimes I even "closed" classrooms due to having no teachers.

I did this!

No one made a room of church attendees clear and scatter like I did when I walked in the door. I was losing friends and am pretty sure had a reputation for being a whiner on my staff team. The truth is, none of it was working and I didn't understand why. I mean, didn't they get how important serving children's ministry is to the vitality of the Church?

I finally went to our executive pastor in tears and told him the dilemma at my campus. He listened thoughtfully and then told me this: "Jana, here's what I want you to do." *Okay— good. He has a plan. I'm ready.*

"I want you and your husband to identify six couples at your church and take them to dinner. Find the ones that you think will really be good at leading others. They are all parents, they want a good children's ministry. Take them to dinner and share your heart for what you do. Tell them all the things about children needing sound teaching, a chance to learn and grow in the Word, a church community that they love, and a partnership with families."

Note: Basically he was saying—challenge them with what you're always challenging us with at staff meeting!

He continued by saying, "Now, once you've cast this great Kingdom-minded vision, then, make 'the ask.' And the ask is this—serve every Sunday for six months." I stopped him right there.

"Kevin, you do not understand. This group won't go for that. It has to be every other week or one month on, one month off—it can't be every week."

He did not change his mind. He prayed for me, smiled, and said, "Trust me, it will work."

I left the office that day and cried all the way home, thinking this will never work, executive pastors don't get children's ministry, my campus has the most unique DNA of any church ever. Not. Gonna. Work. But, I didn't have a plan B. In fact, all my plans had failed me—this was my only shot. I had nothing to lose.

So, my husband, Michael, and I started out on our "dinner campaign." For those of you who are married, you know that your spouse is basically an unpaid staff member. You are in it together because you live it together. And that's exactly where Michael and I found ourselves, God bless him!

Now, it's important to note that "coffee campaigns" are just as effective—and cheaper. They are also easier to find the time, place, and occasion for a quick coffee. What's key to note is the one-to-one ask, or in our case, couple-to-couple.

What happened next? Together we identified couples (remember, most of our church members were young/married couples with multiple children) who showed great potential for being leaders in ministry. Poor guys, they had no idea they were being scouted and basically stalked and eventually "courted" to serve with us.

Where should you look for this kind of leader? Find people who have a passion for evangelism, for discipleship, for expanding God's Kingdom. Basically, you're looking for people who have the same heartbeat for ministry that you do. They may be serving somewhere else, they may have never been asked to serve, or they may think they don't have what it takes. *You* may be the one that speaks that into them. For us, it was young married couples with kids, but there are plenty of other groupings that exist in churches that may fit your context. Single adults, empty nesters, and so forth.

We took each couple out to a casual dinner, enjoyed conversation about church and families, and then simply took some time to share from our heart. We basically cast the vision that has been laid out in the preceding chapters: that we had an urgent burden for the children—the "lambs" amongst us—to know Jesus. We told them that we felt they would be excellent partners to serve alongside us and to help us not only shepherd the children, but to disciple a team of volunteers—to truly help us lead.

We laid out a plan I call "layered discipleship," although at the time we did not give it a name. Since then, I've formed a diagram to represent the model of what we were doing. The six couples whom we personally asked (four of them said yes) to join us would become leaders (we actually called them coaches—some people make this model work with a divisional coordinator). This team would oversee a team of volunteers.

You may be asking—"How are leaders different from volunteers?" A leader is someone that ultimately will report to you as a leader of leaders. Your commitment to them is to pour into their daily lives by sharing their burdens, praying for them, calling or texting them during the week, sharing meals together, and, as much as possible, living life together with a shared, common vision of ministry.

Volunteers are ultimately led by the coaches and become teams. Our volunteers came from a huge pool of college students from one of the other church campuses. Since our campus was in Austin, Texas, we had multiple university students that attended our church. However, there were many who were ready to not just attend but also serve the church, and what better way to develop a college student than to bring them into children's ministry with a loving leader who is ready to "coach" and pour into their daily lives. Do you see how the layers are presenting themselves? Here is a simple diagram to represent this strategy:

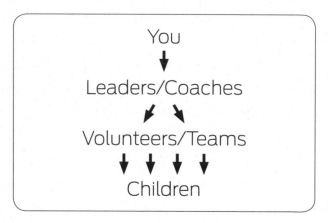

The end goal is to have multiple teams of volunteers who are led by coaches (your leaders). You, as the Kids Ministry Director/Minister/Pastor, become the leader of leaders and they in return develop their teams. If one of their volunteers cannot be there at the last minute, they help find a substitute. Your phone (ideally) should not be blowing up on Saturday night!

When it comes to training, one scenario might be that you train your leaders and they train their teams. Ultimately, the children have trained-up, prayed-up teachers who are ready to serve because they themselves have servant-minded leaders who are developing them.

I realize there are multiple ways to recruit and equip volunteers. This is one strategy that I hope you can find some pieces to make your own. If you only find one take-away, I hope it is this: *multiply yourself by discipling new leaders who can then continue to multiply themselves by developing volunteers who will one day be ready to lead.*

Nourish and serve your leaders and watch how the Lord will use that to expand His Kingdom. I've concluded this chapter with a blog post I wrote a couple of years ago about an added benefit of children seeing their parents serve. I realize it is not the best scenario for all families, but for the ones who can—the results can be amazing and long-lasting. I hope you can use it as a tool to energize the parents in your ministry to serve the church in some capacity.

Why Kids Need to See Their Parents Serve

As a mom and former children's ministry director, I have seen the importance of parents needing to serve the church—both the local church-body and the bigger "C," the body of Christ.

This lesson was revealed to me after hearing "No" countless times when approaching parents to serve in our children's ministry. It wasn't always straight-up no; but, there were plenty of versions of it. For example:

"I don't really know how to teach kids," or

"Sunday mornings are our only time to worship," or my personal favorite,

"Can't the college kids do it?"

Now, before I point the finger at any of these excuses, I must reconcile the fact that I myself have told many a children's director the same things, or hid in the bathroom until they passed by and I could make a clear getaway before being asked to teach the two-year-olds!

The truth is, we live in a culture where church rhythms are changing. For many of us, Sunday morning is the only organized time of meeting on campus while small group meetings are held in homes. Our lives are so busy during the week that we want Sundays to feel like a true Sabbath. We need to ask ourselves, however, "What does not serving communicate to my child?" One must wrestle with the question: if Mom and Dad don't serve the church, will their children do the same when they are older?

One of my favorite memories of my mom is of her sitting in her favorite chair on Saturday nights with her Bible and her lesson, studying to teach her ninth grade girls the next morning. I also remember helping host parties for her girls to come over and eat a meal, do crafts, bake cookies, and so on. She didn't just put in her time on Sunday mornings so the division coordinator would leave her alone, she was truly discipling them and—without even trying—she was preparing me to serve one day. It took me "seeing" her model what serving the body of Christ looked like in order for me to believe that was a calling on my life as I grew into my own spiritual giftings.

We all go through seasons where serving is hard and requires sacrifice. Jesus is worth that sacrifice—and so are our children. We can trust Him to provide rest and Sabbath while we also serve. Whether it is teaching kids, chaperoning a student event, or serving on the parking team, let's remember that little eyes are seeing our actions and believing that they too are called to serve the body of Christ.

Food for Thought Questions

1. Have you struggled with recruitment and enlistment in your ministry? Share a couple of stories.

2. How can you take portions of the "coffee campaign" strategy and make it your own?

3. How can you make the "layered discipleship" concept work for building an army of leaders and volunteers to serve alongside you?

4. Why is it important for kids to see their parents serve the church?

Part 2
_____

Heart Transforming

Essential Nutrient: Healthy Kids Ministry
should be focused on heart transformation,
not behavior modification.

Chapter 7

Essential Nutrient #2: Heart Transforming

"I will give you a new heart and put a new spirit within you; I will remove your heart of stone and give you a heart of flesh."
—EZEKIEL 36:26

Now that we've poured the foundation of what we want our ministries to be—those that are Kingdom Expanding, not simply ministry building—it's time to unpack the second Essential Nutrient: Heart Transforming. This is perhaps the number one reason we felt called to ministry—because we had a burden for children's hearts to be changed by the gospel. We all know this, but implementation can be tricky, especially if we try to make heart change happen through behavior modification—which is impossible.

When we heap behavior modification onto a young soul, we are actually adding a burden, not introducing freedom in Christ. Simply put: Christ has to be at the center of everything we do in Kids Ministry.

When we put Jesus in the center, He will produce the heart transformation that we pray for everyday. In today's world, character education is seen as a valuable tool for children to learn. Public school systems implement curriculum to teach morals and values to their students that are benign from any religious belief system, but are nevertheless "good things" for them to learn. Be kind, don't cheat, don't bully, be a friend, don't do drugs—in a nutshell, make good choices and basically, do the "right thing."

Let's be clear: if what we are teaching our children at church does not look much different from what is taught in our public school systems, then we are not focused on heart transformation—we are focused on behavior modification. To truly be in the heart business, is to truly embrace the fact that only the gospel can transform.

Jesus is the key to changing a heart from stone to flesh and He does it through His Word and the work of the Holy Spirit.

Food for Thought Questions

1. What is the difference between Heart Transformation and Behavior Modification?
2. Explain the pros and the cons of "Character Education."
3. How is a heart transformed?

Chapter 8

Check Yes! Salvation on Paper

"There is salvation in no one else, for there is no other name under heaven given to people, and we must be saved by it."

—ACTS 4:12

I was saved at Vacation Bible School at age nine. It was on a Thursday, the day where the gospel presentation was given by the pastor, and children were given the opportunity to respond. For me, that opportunity was given in the form of a question on a piece of paper with a box to check yes or no.

"Are you interested in learning more about becoming a Christian? Check Yes or No." I was the child of a minister on staff at our church. I had heard about Jesus all of my life, but this was the first time I had the urge to "check yes." So, I did and my parents were called and told by the church secretary. They talked to me more when I returned home and, later that night, I prayed to receive Jesus as my Savior and Lord.

Now, that is my story. I do believe it was Spirit-led, but I do believe it began way before the check-box moment.

Why?

Because I had been exposed to the Word for years and years before, preparing a fertile heart for the Spirit to move "for such a time as this." There is no doubt that was the moment I trusted Jesus, and I am so grateful for the VBS experience that led to it.

What concerns me is that not all of our children are ready for the check-box experience—also known as "close your eyes and raise your hand" or "stay after class if you want to ask

Jesus in your heart." I am concerned that we corner kids into making a decision that the Holy Spirit may not be leading them to make, yet. We also use language that may not make sense—my own eight-year-old is still trying to understand the literal part of "Jesus in your heart."

For the most part, children love structure (and even rules). If we make the salvation experience too much like a checklist, we may get some false positives. One may ask, "Isn't it better to get kids to make professions of faith at an early age and let the Holy Spirit work later?" My humble answer to that is "no" and here is why.

Another scary statistic that we hear too often is about church kids not returning to the church after leaving home (or returning home). There are too many signs pointing to kids "leaving the faith." If they can "leave the faith," then you have to ask yourself, were they ever truly saved? Did Jesus transform their hearts? Or, were they just checking "yes" at VBS?

It is something with which we must wrestle.

As we seek to partner with parents and caregivers to truly disciple a child's heart, it's important that both families and churches understand that, ultimately, our God is in control. He calls our children to Himself in His own time. We can teach them the gospel and, more importantly, display the gospel to them, but cannot transform their hearts on our own.

Neither parents nor the Church can push a child into the faith. Daniel Darling of the Ethics and Religious Liberty Commission states:

> Putting all the pressure on parents to execute and then blaming only them for failure is both unbiblical and impossible. Unbiblical because it removes the work of God and brings glory to man. Impossible because human parents cannot manufacture what only the Holy Spirit can produce. We forget that every child is an individual human soul, created with their own accountability before God. Worse, we ignore the work of the Holy Spirit in the shaping of a child's soul. So what is the job of a parent? Faithfulness. Parents are given the task of creating a culture of faith that intentionally uses all of life to point their children toward a lifelong relationship with God. We're to equip them

for life. But the job of conversion and sanctification can only be done by God through the work of the Holy Spirit. Only God can shape the human heart. Too many Christian parenting models operate under the subtle assumption that the life, death and resurrection of Jesus Christ is incidental to parenting. But gospel parenting is more than simply hoping our kids nod in affirmation at the offer of the gospel in Sunday school. Gospel parenting frees us from taking the place of God.[4]

As a leader in your church and Kids Ministry, I encourage you to equip your leaders and volunteer teams as well as the families you steward to present the gospel as often as they can, but with faithfulness to wait upon the Lord and His perfect timing.

Food for Thought Questions

1. How can we encourage parents and ministry leaders to be careful not to push children into belief?

2. What are some ways we can provide appropriate opportunities for a child to respond to the gospel?

3. How can we equip families to create a culture of faith that points children toward a personal relationship with Jesus?

Chapter 9

Heretical Me: The Danger of Haphazard Discipleship

Then God said, "Let Us make man in Our image, according to Our likeness."
—Genesis 1:26

*D*iscipleship is such a sticky word right now in circles of ministry. We all know that evangelism is essential to our calling as followers of Jesus and as Kids Ministry leaders; we know the urgency of leading our children to Christ. However, there is such thing as discipleship in congruence with evangelism—not just what you do after a child becomes a believer. In fact, discipleship actually includes evangelism (see Matt. 28:19–20). That is why it is so important that your ministry has a wise plan of discipleship—one that is age appropriate for each stage of a child's life both mentally and spiritually.

Think about it for a second, you oversee multiple age groups (depending on your job description). Some of you are over "only" preschool ministry or "only" children's ministry. But even within those two age groups, several more exist. I believe there are at least six developmental phases in childhood: Younger Preschoolers (babies–2s), Middle Preschoolers (3s and 4s), Older Preschoolers (Pre-K–Kindergarten), Younger Kids (grades 1–2), Middle Kids (grades 3–4), and Preteens (grades 5–6). These groupings are fluid, and churches move age groups around according to church context and even space. For example, some churches put Kindergarten with Preschool and some place them with younger children. Some Kids Ministries don't have 6th grade and some do. The point is, there are roughly six developmental stages that are represented in Kids Ministry—from babes in arms when they come to us, to braces and acne when they leave us for Student/Youth ministry. That's a lot of development and precisely why a very thought-out discipleship plan is necessary for what you do. It's important to note that a discipleship plan is different from a curriculum. Before you select a curriculum, it's necessary to have a roadmap for where you are going—that would be a discipleship plan.

My background (before ministry) and college major was in Interdisciplinary Studies—which is another way to say I have a degree in Education. (I always have to explain that when someone sees my diploma!) As a teacher, I had goals and objectives that were essential for children to achieve before they could move onto the next grade. These were so important to the state of Texas that they were written in detail on large posters and given to me as a public school teacher to hang on my wall so that they were in front of me at all times.

I taught 4th grade, but also included on my poster were 3rd grade skills and 5th grade skills so that I could know what my students had already mastered and know what they were going to need to master in the next grade. It was a plan to be used so that if I had kids who needed to catch up, I had those third grade skills to look at. If I had a student who was ready to move on, I had the 5th grade plan right in front of me to know what was next.

This was a roadmap for me to know where we were headed and what the ultimate goals would be. I could not teach from it, however. I had to have curriculum that would help support and accomplish these goals. I use this as a parallel to show how in ministry, we should have a spiritual roadmap of where kids are in each developmental stage of their childhood. A free resource that our LifeWay Kids team developed is called Levels of Biblical Learning,[5] based on years of theological and pedagogical research from experts in ministry and education. Again, it is not a curriculum—or even a scope and sequence or study plan. It lists what a child in each of the six age groups is capable of learning spiritually. And because you have multiple ages listed, there will be room to go back and forth depending on a child's readiness.

If we do not have a plan like this in place, it can be all too easy to fall into what I call "haphazard discipleship." This kind of discipleship happens when you cherry-pick content to teach Bible stories and hope that the child gets what he or she needs from it. It's tempting to gravitate to this style of discipleship—after all, free content for teaching Bible stories can be found on Google in seconds. Activities and crafts can be freely found on Pinterest. We can piece-meal together biblical content to create a make-shift discipleship plan, but if not careful, it ends up being haphazard and can even lead to kids not receiving a full understanding of biblical concepts. Haphazard is one H word I use for this, but I could use another one as a warning: heretical. If we don't have a spiritual roadmap for what kids are learning, they could inadvertently be learning heretical things. I will use myself as an example here. I grew up in a Christian home, in great churches that were theologically sound. I have no idea what discipleship plan was used in my childhood kids ministry or youth ministry. I remember learning Bible stories, I remember understanding that Jesus loved me and had a plan for me, and like I said in an earlier chapter, I remember saying yes to a relationship with Him. However, I did *not* understand that the Bible was one story about God.

I could say the books of the Bible, but I didn't know that they all had a purpose that worked together—and that Scripture proved Scripture time and time again. I could tell you that the Trinity meant God, three in one. But, it wasn't until I was in my late twenties that I understood that Jesus was present at creation. In my little mind, God *created* Jesus and sent Him to save us. Folks, that is heresy. No one taught me that, but that is what my brain wove together based on what I was (or was not) taught. No one set out to teach me these things, but that is the danger of not having a wise discipleship plan that helps children navigate and learn the spiritual concepts that are necessary to learn and grow in God's Word.

I am so grateful that God used all the things I was taught as a child to eventually bring a solid theologically sound backbone in His perfect timing. But, let's give our children the kind of discipleship that can help avoid this kind of example.

The Levels of Biblical Learning, as mentioned before, are based on six age levels (three in preschool and three kids groups) but are also centered around ten concept areas, or categories: God, Jesus, Holy Spirit, Bible, Salvation, Creation, Church, People, Family, and Community and World.

I often receive questions about how do you "teach" a young preschooler about the Holy Spirit? Clearly, the Holy Spirit is an abstract concept, so we don't necessarily teach them with those words—yet. However, this tool lays out statements that tell you what a two-year-old might understand that would lay foundations for learning about the Holy Spirit as they are ready.

For example, they can learn that "God loves me" and that "God helps me." By the time the child is in preteen years, they are understanding statements such as: "The Trinity has always existed." (Remember how I missed that one as a child?) It's all spelled out in this special document that I hope you will use to train your volunteers, equip your parents, and disciple the children in your ministry.

A healthy Kids Ministry that truly nourishes will have a plan in place to help children grow in God's Word at every stage of childhood.

Food for Thought Questions

1. Do you have a wise discipleship plan in place for your ministry?

2. How can a tool like the Levels of Biblical Learning help as you disciple children from very young until they leave for the student ministry?

3. Do you have any haphazard or accidental heretical discipleship in your past? Share a few examples.

Chapter 10

The Velcro Gospel: Attachment Teaching

"For God loved the world in this way: He gave His One and Only Son, so that everyone who believes in Him will not perish but have eternal life."
—JOHN 3:16

John 3:16. This is the verse that captures the gospel so succinctly. People hold signs up at sporting events and rallies—hoping that someone might see it and look it up on the Internet or in a Bible they may have and latch on to its saving message. Christian businesses place it on their shopping bags or marquees. It is a powerful verse and one that children should learn from a young age. But, it's not the only way to present the gospel.

Heart Transformation happens when we center our teaching on the gospel. To some, this means teach a Bible story and then tell the plan of salvation. I call this attachment teaching—almost using the gospel like a piece of Velcro that we tack on at the end of a lesson. I can't tell you that there is anything terribly wrong, per se, with this style of teaching.

But we should ask ourselves, is there a better way?

Let's use Noah's ark as an example. When we tell preschoolers and kids this favorite story (which is ironic that we decorate children's areas with animals and rainbows, in spite of it being one of the most violent stories in the Bible), we usually focus on Noah obeying God by building an enormous boat in spite of drought conditions and people endlessly teasing him, God keeping Noah and his family safe during the flood while the rest of humanity drowned, and God making His promise to Noah to never again flood the entire earth.

Sometimes after we tell a story like this, we want to close by "attaching" the plan of salvation or John 3:16, but not making the connection of how those two things relate.

Again, I call this the Velcro gospel method, and I've been one to use this strategy before. It's tempting because we want to share the gospel as often as we can in Kids Ministry. But, place yourself on a carpet square in the story circle for a minute and listen through the ears of a 2nd grader: Noah, God, and Jesus died for your sins. Could this be confusing? Yes. There is a better way.

Now, don't hear me say, "We can't mix the Old and New Testaments," because that is not true at all. Some seasoned teachers say it will confuse a child if we talk about both in the same lesson. This represents a completely different style of teaching—one that would not talk about Jesus in the same session as Noah and God. So, the gospel is saved for New Testament stories to avoid confusion. I call this the separatist method.

Gospel-centered teaching is neither of the above. It's not the Velcro method and it's not the separatist method.

Gospel-centered teaching is, however, the best way to teach children of all ages. Let's have another look at Noah with a gospel-centric view.

> One day, God looked at all the people on the earth and saw that every thought was evil and full of sin. He was sorry that He had ever made man. So God said, "I will wipe man off the face of the earth."
>
> But Noah was a good and righteous man who tried to follow God in all things. . . . God wanted to save Noah, so He said to him, "Build an ark out of gopher wood. . . . I will flood the earth, and everything on it will die. But I will keep you safe. You will go into the ark with your sons, your wife, and your sons' wives. Take with you two of every living creature, male and female, to keep them alive too."
>
> So Noah built the ark just as God told him. Then he, his family, and the animals went inside, and God shut the door. The rains came, and it rained for 40 days and 40 nights. The waters rose and covered the entire earth—even the mountains! Everything on dry

land died. Only Noah and those in the ark lived. For 150 days, the water completely covered the earth.

Then God sent a wind to dry up the waters. . . . Noah . . . sent out a raven. The raven flew back and forth until the waters dried up. Then Noah sent out a dove, but she came back to the ark because she couldn't find a place to rest. After seven days, Noah sent the dove out again. This time she came back with an olive leaf. A week later, Noah sent the dove out again, and this time she didn't return. The ground was dry.

Noah, his family, and all the animals came out of the ark. God promised He would never again flood the whole earth. Then He placed a rainbow in the sky as a sign of His promise.[6]

Okay, so we all know this foundational Bible story. But, ask yourself—why is this a key, foundational story that we should teach children? How do we connect Noah to Jesus without slapping on the Velcro gospel? Here is what we do not want kids to miss—the Christ Connection:

The story of the flood shows us how serious God is about sin. He will not leave sin unpunished. But the story of Noah also shows us how loving God is. He provided a rescue plan for one righteous man—Noah. The rescue was extended to Noah's family. This story points ahead to a greater rescue! Jesus, the only perfectly righteous person, came to take the punishment for sin. We trust His act of obedience and are saved from the punishment our sin deserves.[7]

When children understand how the Bible is one Big Story about God's plan, then the process of heart transformation can begin. When they truly understand that they are a sinner, which separates them from God, but that they can be with

God forever through the gift He gave us in Jesus, then they can respond to the gospel by saying yes to Jesus. A powerful tool that our team likes to use is *The Gospel: God's Plan for Me.*[8] I hope you can use it to train volunteers and parents as they pray and teach these precious souls with the hope and goal of true heart transformation. Nourish the kids in your ministry with gospel-centered teaching and pray with faithfulness that God will call them to Himself in His perfect timing.

Food for Thought Questions

1. How were you taught the gospel as a child and teen? Did it seem like a Velcro gospel presentation? Share your story.

2. How can we teach young children Old Testament stories, but with a connection to Christ, without confusing them?

3. How will you train your volunteers and parents to focus on gospel-centered teaching in order to produce true heart transformation?

THE GOSPEL

GOD'S PLAN for US

The gospel is the good news, the message about Christ, the kingdom of God, and salvation. Use these prompts to share the gospel with your kids.

GOD RULES.

Ask: "Who is in charge at home?" Explain that because God created everything, He is in charge of everything.
Read Revelation 4:11.

WE SINNED.

Ask: "Have you ever done something wrong?" Tell kids that everyone sins, or disobeys God. Our sin separates us from God.
Read Romans 3:23.

GOD PROVIDED.

Explain that God is holy and must punish sin. God sent His Son, Jesus, to take the punishment we deserve.
Read John 3:16.

JESUS GIVES.

Ask: "What is the best gift you've ever received?" Say that Jesus took our punishment for sin by giving His life, and He gives us His righteousness. God sees us as if we lived the perfect life Jesus lived. This is the best gift ever! Read 2 Corinthians 5:21.

WE RESPOND.

Explain that everyone has a choice to make. Ask: "Will you trust Jesus as your Savior and Lord? You can turn from self and sin and turn to Jesus." Read Romans 10:9-10.

Chapter 11

Behavior Modification: Quick Fix vs. God's Grace

Train up a child in the way he should go, and
when he is old he will not depart from it.
—PROVERBS 22:6

I am a mom of three babies. Okay, so they are not really babies anymore and by the time this book is out, they will have grown even more. I have one daughter in middle school, one preteen son, and one elementary son. I love motherhood—but let's face it, the actual parenting part is just hard!

I am a trained educator and have worked with kids nearly all my life—especially through the lens of ministry. Even as a teen I was a camp counselor in the summers and taught VBS in Central America on mission trips. All this experience, yet my own precious three can bring me to my knees for two reasons: crying mercy and begging God for help.

This is where I sometimes get caught in the trap of wanting behavior change, even before heart change. Why? Because it is quicker, it's results-driven, and quite frankly, I just need obedience—now!

But, if I'm honest, I know that a quick demand for obedience is only a Band-Aid for true heart transformation, which only God can accomplish. My role as a parent is to live out the gospel so that they can see that I, too, sin, mess up, and fail them because I am a sinner in need of a rescuer just like they are. My role is to model grace for them just like God has so lavishly given us grace upon grace. When my husband and I let go and parent with heart transformation in mind rather than the quick-fix expectation of behavior change, we automatically feel a peace in our home. Something that is centered upon loving and serving one another as a response to how our heavenly Father has loved us and provided a way for us to be with Him forever.

So, that's on a good day. Another trap that I fall into is the desire that, above all, my kids will be gracious (good manners), accomplished (well-rounded) leaders (great character). My intentions are good, I assure you.

You see, I am raising American kids. There is a high expectation that they will be good at school, sports, music, and charity so that they can get a scholarship into a great college! As parents, we all live with this pressure because we are all playing the game. But sometimes, the Lord so tenderly pulls me back and let's me see a bigger picture. There is no way, try as I might, to force all of these things to happen. I can teach my kids about morals and values, but that is not the silver bullet for heart transformation. Again, it is about raising kids who love Jesus. I can point the way and the Church can partner with me (which is why your job is so important), but heart change begins with teaching the Bible, not teaching manners and character development.

Heart transformation can lead to behavior modification, but not the other way around. It is key for ministry leaders to understand this. Just like my confessions of bad parenting, there are countless examples of how the Church is also tempted to pile on behavior modification tactics, expecting them to lead to heart transformation. If morals and values are the only thing you are teaching, then you take away the power of the cross.

We need to realize that when we do this, we are adding a burden that children can't fix on their own—they will never be able to obey enough, perform enough, or not mess up enough. The list of values we want to see championed in their lives will be fleeting if the Holy Spirit is not producing the fruit of the Spirit. They need a Savior.

To truly nourish the hearts of children in your ministry, Christ has to be at the center of all that we do. He is the only one who can produce true heart transformation.

Food for Thought Questions

1. Are you ever tempted to lean more heavily on expecting behavior modification in children?

2. How are we as a society heaping on extra burdens to our children that they will never measure up to?

3. How can the Church be more effective in ministry by focusing on heart transformation, leaning on the timing of the Holy Spirit for each child?

Part 3

Culture Shaping

Essential Nutrient: Healthy Kids Ministry should be focused on bringing up a generation of culture-shaping kids, not kids who are shaped by the culture.

Chapter 12

Essential Nutrient #3: Culture Shaping

*Like arrows in the hands of a warrior
are the sons born in one's youth.*
—PSALM 127:4

The Essential Nutrients are meant to be in a certain order, though they can stand alone. If you look at the sequence that they are revealed in this book, you can see that there is a trajectory of some sort. In essence, it is important to get the first one right before moving along to the next. That said, they must all three work together simultaneously. If we return to the analogy of essential nutrients in food, you will recall that the physical body must have essential nutrients to function and it cannot synthesize these nutrients on its own. They must come from the diet. Applied to ministry, we can provide these essentials to make sure our Kids Ministries are healthy and thriving.

Let's review where we have been so far and where we are headed next:

- We have discussed how to prepare a Kingdom Expanding vision and foundation for your Kids Ministry, not simply a ministry building focused on counting attendance and filling spots.

- We've learned how to focus on a Heart Transforming mind-set as opposed to behavior modifying outcomes that become more about morals and values, rather than gospel-centered transformation.

- The next Essential Nutrient for a healthy Kids Ministry that must be addressed is how to bring up Culture Shaping warriors! I love the verse that describes this essential, which is why an arrow icon was chosen to pictorially represent a Culture Shaping ministry.

By the time kids leave us after the 5th or 6th grade, we want them to be prepared to engage the culture surrounding them in a powerful, impactful way. Just like a sharpened arrow in the hands of a skilled archer, we want to launch them to make a difference in the world because they have been rooted in Scripture and transformed by Christ. If our arrows are dull, they won't be able to penetrate the darkness. Our prayer is that our kids have already come to know Jesus as their Savior and are now being led by the Holy Spirit, so that they may be disciples who are ready to go make more disciples of their friends, neighbors, classmates, and beyond.

On the contrary, we don't want to see them shaped by the culture. Unfortunately, the kids we serve are inheriting a very dark culture that includes things that we as leaders have not had to navigate before. The world desperately needs a generation to be the "salt and light" that will bring more people into God's Kingdom. While it sounds overwhelming, it's exciting that God has called us to make these young disciples into world changers, culture shapers, and ultimately leaders.

Food for Thought Questions

1. Review the definition of an Essential Nutrient and describe the analogy as applied to ministry.

2. What does the theme verse of this chapter mean to you? How can you use it to unleash a Culture Shaping Kids Ministry?

3. What cultural dynamics concern you or even frighten you when it comes to releasing the kids in your ministry to be the salt and light the world needs?

Chapter 13

Moonlight Towers: Illuminating Dark Spaces

Then Jesus spoke to them again: "I am the light of the world. Anyone who follows Me will never walk in the darkness but will have the light of life."
—JOHN 8:12

My husband, Michael, and I began our marriage and started a family in the amazing city of Austin, Texas. It was our home for sixteen years and it will always be very close to our hearts for many reasons. One reason is that this is where God began weaving His story of my career path. I began my teaching career there, but after four short years in the classroom, God called me to something I could never have dreamed up on my own.

As a 4th grade teacher in the public school system, I was charged with the task to teach Texas History. (Ask any Texan and they know that 4th and 7th grades are dedicated to educating the children of Texas about their great state!) Well, I absolutely *loved* teaching it. I am a bit of a history buff and had lived in Texas my entire life, and—let's all admit—Texas is the greatest state ever (I can feel eyes roll as I write this; I apologize—all the states are great)!

The principal of my school at the time knew I was passionate about teaching Texas history, so she submitted my name as a candidate to be on a committee that would advise a brand-new museum being built by the Texas legislature. This would be no ordinary, dusty history museum—that's not how Texas does things. It would be an enormous, state-of-the-art facility located right next to the state capitol and made with the same granite from the same quarry that the capitol itself is made of. The best part of this museum would be its mission and dedication to the children, teachers, and families of Texas to learn in an engaging way through the power of story. Thus, the title of the museum is the Texas State History Museum, but the tag line is: The Story of Texas.

I was honored to be on the committee of educators that would advise the museum about opening its own education department. Little did I know at the time, I would ultimately be on staff as an educator who would write and develop programming, curriculum, and exhibit design for teachers to use with their classrooms and families to enjoy together. It was a dream job. A blending of all the things I loved. God used this time in my life to plant seeds that would blossom into a heart for the culture I lived in and an urgency to see that culture know Him. I was beginning to learn what being a culture shaper really meant.

Another reason our time in Austin was so special is that we had the opportunity to help a young pastor and his wife begin a church plant at a middle school in our neighborhood. I'll never forget when we were still visiting the vision meetings and gatherings, deciding if we would jump in this adventure of planting a church, the pastor, Zac Allen, gave a sermon using moonlight towers as an illustration.

What is a moonlight tower, you might ask? They are historic lighting structures from the late 1800s used to illuminate areas of a town or city at night. The special thing about Austin moonlight towers is that they are the only ones in the world that have been maintained and still work—and are used today all over town. These structures are huge—165 feet tall with a base of 15 feet and can illuminate a 1,500-foot circle bright enough to read a watch!

The sermon illustration was really a way to cast a vision for what he wanted this brand-new little church to do—to inspire its members to symbolically go be a moonlight tower in your own neighborhood. Well, that resonated with me—my ears perked up when I heard about these historical masterpieces unique only to my beloved city and state. But, to then be charged with the task of reaching our own neighborhood was both energizing and overwhelming.

The rest of Texas might be considered the Bible Belt, but the city of Austin certainly is not. In fact, it is generally considered to be at least 80 percent unchurched and by the time I write this, that statistic will change as Austin is a boom city with unprecedented growth and a post-modern cultural flair. The thought of being a light to our neighborhood seemed hopeless. Our street alone had most of the world religions represented (Buddhism, Islam, and Judaism) and the rest were agnostic or atheist. How could we reach them? This was not the "invite to Sunday School" kind of crew.

But, I hooked onto the message. I visited the moonlight towers, researched them, and learned more about what they really did. Originally they were installed to be light in dark areas. There were no street lights, and gas lamps weren't effective enough to bring large groups together. With the moonlight towers, several blocks at a time had light. So, people of the town would gravitate to the light for social functions, town meetings, and who knows? Maybe even host church. One can only imagine.

The point of this chapter is to give you some context of what has to happen to engage the culture. For me, God used the history of my state to show me that there were plenty of dark spaces that needed light and that my family had a role in providing light to the people in our lives. How can the Church be the moonlight tower in our communities, towns, and cities?

I tell you these stories to begin to unpack what it truly means for kids to be culture shapers. How can the kids in your ministry be the light to the countless people that they will know the rest of their lives? It is our role to teach them that Jesus calls us no matter what our age is—to go make disciples! The Great Commission is not just for teens and adults.

And the honest truth is, in order to fulfill the Great Commission, we must illuminate dark spaces. When our kids shine the light of Christ, darkness cannot help but disappear. And just like our church plant encouraged us to start with our neighbors, our kids can start with their friends, neighbors, sports teams, and anyone else they are living life with.

As a resource, I've provided a tool that we have called "How to Lead a Friend to Christ." This of course would only be for older children who have confessed their faith in Jesus and are ready to understand how to share the gospel.

My prayer is that you would use it to spur on young hearts for evangelism. Kids who are nourished with the gospel will have an overflowing of love for their lost friends and communities.

Food for Thought Questions

1. Describe the culture you live in—what are some of its unique attributes?
2. How can your church and Kids Ministry engage the culture by illuminating the darkness?
3. Why must we help kids understand their role in the Great Commission?

Tips When Talking to a Friend about Becoming a Christian

* Once you feel God leading you to talk with someone about Jesus, begin to pray for that person by name and ask God to give you an opportunity to talk with this friend or family member about your faith in Jesus.
* Be sure you are familiar with the ABCs of Becoming a Christian tract or the tear-off leaflet of this booklet, "Leading a Friend to Christ."
* Simply share what you believe the Bible teaches about God and Jesus. Don't worry that you are not a preacher. Sometimes a friend will listen to you more quickly than to a church helper.
* Talk just as if you are carrying on a conversation.
* Try not to argue with your friend/family member. All you need to do is tell what the Bible teaches and let God do the work of helping your friend or family member understand and want to have a personal relationship with God.
* Even if your friend or family member doesn't seem interested in becoming a Christian, you can share what God has done for you and what He wants to do for every person on earth.
* Have extra copies of the ABCs of Becoming a Christian tract so that you can give your friend or family member his very own copy.
* NEVER feel unsuccessful if your friend does not choose to pray and invite Jesus into his life. Be faithful in telling others about Jesus. God is the One who helps people understand who He is and that He has a plan for their lives.

How to Become a Christian

ADMIT

ADMIT TO GOD THAT YOU ARE A SINNER. THE FIRST PEOPLE GOD CREATED CHOSE TO SIN AND DISOBEY GOD. EVER SINCE THEN, ALL PEOPLE HAVE CHOSEN TO SIN AND DISOBEY.

* Romans 3:23–Underline this verse in your Bible.

REPENT, TURN AWAY FROM YOUR SIN.

* Acts 3:19; 1 John 1:9–Underline these verses in your Bible.

BELIEVE

BELIEVE THAT JESUS IS GOD'S SON AND ACCEPT GOD'S GIFT OF FORGIVENESS FROM SIN.

* Acts 16:31; Acts 4:12; John 14:6; Ephesians 2:8-9–Underline these verses in your Bible.

CONFESS

CONFESS YOUR FAITH IN JESUS CHRIST AS SAVIOR AND LORD.

* Romans 10:9-10,13–Underline these verses in your Bible.
* If the child is ready, he can pray a prayer like this to God:

Dear God,
I know I have sinned and my sin separates me from You. I am sorry for my sin. I believe Jesus died on the cross for me so my sin can be forgiven. I believe Jesus rose from the dead and is alive. God, please forgive me. I ask Jesus to come into my life and be my Savior and Lord. I will obey You and live for You the rest of my life. Thank You. In Jesus' name I pray, Amen.

Chapter 14

Hayrides and Hotdogs: Missional Family Ministry

"You are the light of the world. A city situated on a hill cannot be hidden."
—MATTHEW 5:14

If we want a Kids Ministry that truly nourishes, then we must reach the family, which I believe is something that all Kids Ministry leaders can agree on. A nourishing family yields more fruit than a family that is not healthy or equipped enough to disciple their child. This is not to say that a family has to be perfect in order to live a life on mission—we all know that families are messy. But, we want parents to understand that in spite of the messiness and sin in their own lives, the gospel is big enough to transform whole families. These are the families that have a Kingdom Expanding mind-set, a focus on Heart Transforming discipleship, and who desire to make an impact on the culture they live in.

There is no better way for kids to see how to engage the culture than to watch it being modeled by their parents. So, the question is: how do we foster this mind-set in our Kids Ministries? How do we equip and unleash parents to live on mission as families? For my family, it started with an idea and challenge from our church.

Go back to Austin, Texas, with me again: same church plant, same pastor, same neighborhood. With the "moonlight tower" concept guiding our way, my husband and I decided to host a cookout on Halloween. The church would not be hosting a Fall Festival—in fact, it was the church leadership who charged all of the families to go spend Halloween in our own neighborhoods. After all, it's one of the only times all year when all of your neighbors will come to your house, whether you invite them or not. Think about it: no pressure to do the most difficult part of outreach—*inviting*.

In order to spread the gospel, you have to know people, right? And, in order to share your faith, you need to have some sort of established relationship. It was time for us to get to know our neighbors, and we were going to take advantage of this moment when everyone would pass by our house.

So, we got the kids to help us. We made a trip to Costco and bought hotdogs, chips, and paper goods in bulk. We drug our grill out in the driveway, set up a few tables and camp chairs, turned on some music—and waited. Would anyone come? Slowly but surely, little costumed children in red wagons, moms, dads, empty nesters, a few teens, and even guests from other neighborhoods came to our front yard party. My kids got to meet new friends and by the end of the evening, we were all having fun together. E-mails and phone numbers were collected and, for the first time, we felt like we knew everyone living around us.

From that first party, neighborhood play groups were launched for preschoolers and moms, carpools to school started for grade-schoolers, and a ladies' book club began meeting monthly. Instead of living life beside each other, we began doing life together. As I mentioned in the previous chapter, Austin is a diverse group of people with multiple belief systems. This approach gave us the relational capital we would need to have engaging conversations that could usher in gospel conversations.

Fast-forward one year later and we decided to hitch our small trailer on the back of my husband's old blue Jeep, grab some hay bales, and add a hayride to the now annual Halloween party. Every year more families joined us to help and more families came to the festivities. Just recently, our closest friends who helped us start the very first one almost ten years ago told us that the party had grown to a full-blown block party with the entire street blocked, a food truck, inflatables, and more people than ever attending.

What I love most about this story is that it began with kids. I mean adults don't go asking for candy door-to-door unless they have kids (well, they shouldn't, at least). No, we wanted to help our kids celebrate a fun part of the fall season—if you don't like calling it "Halloween," Fall Festivals are widely accepted as an alternate name. Don't let that cause you to miss a time when everyone is out and knocking on each other's doors! Face it, that would be weird any other time!

In order to have Culture Shaping kids, we need to get moms, dads, grandparents, and caregivers involved. Share stories like mine and see if it spurs on some creativity in the lives of your church family. I have heard about people starting hot chocolate and caroling parties and/or cookie swaps at Christmas time. I have heard about neighborhood Easter egg hunts or just a simple cookout on the 4th of July or a crawfish boil in the summer. The power of story is so important to acknowledge when you are trying to engage your families in missional living. Share how people in your church are living on mission in your weekly communication and encourage them to get involved in living on mission with their children. As Christians, we need to know some nonbelievers in order to spread the gospel. If we only surround ourselves with people who are just like us, then we are neglecting the Great Commission and our children are not seeing it modeled for them.

From these entry-point kinds of parties and events, it is easier to launch more evangelical kinds of initiatives. My daughter and I had the opportunity to start a Backyard Bible Club with the girls in her grade. Many churches provide materials for families to do Backyard VBS in the summer—or really anytime.

Challenge the families in your midst to live on mission together! Give them tools, ideas, and stories and then just pray and watch. I guarantee they will latch on and make it their own. To bring up Culture Shaping Kids, you, leader, must incorporate missional living in your Kids Ministry culture.

Food for Thought Questions

1. How can we foster a Culture Shaping mind-set in the families we serve in our ministry?

2. Why is it so important for children to see the Great Commission modeled for them at home?

3. What are some ways you can begin to incorporate missional family ministry into how you lead?

Chapter 15

Balancing Act: Protecting and Preparing Our Kids

Guard your heart above all else,
for it is the source of life.
—PROVERBS 4:23

In order for your Kids Ministry to embrace the culture, it's important to acknowledge that they will encounter some things that we may not be ready for them to see, hear, or experience. The truth is, many children will already be exposed to pornographic images before they leave your ministry. They know about homosexuality, gay marriage, and transgender issues. Your job is not to teach them about these things, but you can make sure that they are equipped with biblically and doctrinally sound teaching to form what they do believe. This goes back to having a wise discipleship plan in place. Kids should be prepared to defend the sanctity of human life, the sanctity of marriage being between one man and one woman, and that we are all made in the image of God. See the Levels of Biblical Learning for statements that help teach these truths appropriately at every stage of childhood.

Parents are looking to the Church for help to navigate the unprecedented situations that their children are encountering. You can assist families by helping them understand that there is a balance between protecting kids while at the same time preparing them. We can certainly protect kids by using software for Internet protection, monitoring their screen time, and using discretion when choosing movies, music, electronic games, and media in general. Extra diligence will be needed when kids begin using social media. There are many resources that can help you be prepared for this kind of equipping.

While protecting, even over-protecting, will come natural to parents, we need to be mindful that all the protecting in the world will never keep our children from being exposed to our culture. It is our role to also prepare them to encounter things in our culture that are contradictory to what they have been taught. Russell Moore, in his book *Onward: Engaging the Culture without Losing the Gospel,* states,

> The church now has the opportunity to bear witness in a culture that often does not even pretend to share our "values." That is not a tragedy since we were never given a mission to promote "values" in the first place, but to speak instead of sin and of righteousness and judgment, of Christ and his kingdom. We will now have to articulate concepts we previously assumed—concepts such as "marriage" and "family" and "faith" and "religion."
>
> So much the better, since Jesus and the apostles do the same thing, defining these categories in terms of the creation and of the gospel. We should have been doing such all along. Now we will be forced to,

simply to be understood at all. Our end goal is not a Christian America, either of the made-up past or the hoped-for future. Our end goal is the kingdom of Christ, made up of every tribe, tongue, nation, and language.[9]

This book is excellent for equipping yourself about the culture we live in so that you can help families navigate these issues. Another resource is the Ethics and Religious Liberty Commission website—www.ERLC.org—the very agency where Russell Moore is President. It is full of free resources that can be shared with parents who are desperate to understand how to bring up kids who will not be "conformed to this age, but be transformed by the renewing of [their] mind" (Rom. 12:2).

A healthy Kids Ministry will equip parents to not be fearful of having difficult conversations with their children about the scary things in our culture. There has never been a more important time to be rooted in Scripture than now. Statistics tell us that children and adults are more biblically illiterate than ever. If we don't know what the Scriptures say, then it becomes very difficult to talk to kids about the questions they have about our culture. Urge your parents to stay in the Word. Talk to other ministry leaders to form a well-balanced plan for families to stay connected and engaged in order to strengthen conversations at home.

Healthy Kids Ministries are diligent with the sword of the Spirit—God's Word—to equip children and parents to impact the culture with a solid biblical response.

Food for Thought Questions

1. What issues in our culture today concern you most when it comes to helping kids know how to be Culture Shapers?

2. How can you sharpen the "arrows" in your ministry to make sure they are biblically sound?

3. How can you equip parents to navigate and be prepared to shepherd their children through cultural dynamics?

Chapter 16

A Heart for the Nations: Bringing Up Senders and Goers

"Go, therefore, and make disciples, baptizing them in the name of the Father, the Son, and the Holy Spirit, teaching them to observe everything I have commanded you. And remember, I am with you always, to the end of the age."
—MATTHEW 28:19–20

Traditionally, most evangelical churches have placed a big emphasis on missions education for children and teens. I am grateful for the time I spent in Mission Friends and Girls in Action (and my brother is grateful for his time in Royal Ambassadors). These programs, which taught thousands about global missions through resources and programming, are important for children to begin hearing the stories of missionaries in their communities and around the world. It's also important for them to learn about giving at an early age so that as they grow, they will not think that supporting missionaries is a "foreign" concept.

I am continually grateful for the International Mission Board (IMB) and the work they do for missions education through their Web-based program Kids on Mission[10] and for the North American Mission Board (NAMB) capturing stories of church planting across the US and Canada. Our team at LifeWay Kids is passionate about including IMB and NAMB, as well as other missions organizations in the videos we include with our Bible studies for kids. It is our view that children should be exposed to the need for prayer, giving, and action around the world at every opportunity possible. Since more families attend weekly worship and Bible study than a second hour during the week (where missions education traditionally takes place in some churches), it's important that we share local and international stories about missionaries in all that we do—including the primary teaching hour, be it Sunday morning, Saturday night, or whenever churches meet.

That being said, I don't think stories and programming are always enough for kids to truly catch the vision and urgency of the Great Commission. It needs to be in the DNA of the Church, in Kids Ministry, and the leaders and volunteers who are teaching our children. We also need to put missionaries in front of our kids regularly. If we can blend a teacher who also has experience as a missionary to speak into our kids, that's the real win.

The Austin Stone Community Church, where I was on staff most recently, has an incredible program for equipping and sending missionaries all over the world. As a Kids Minister, I had the benefit of these missionaries-in-training to be some of my best leaders and teachers. What better place for someone who has a heart for evangelism to be than in the fertile soil of children's ministry. I could cry as I write this, but the very best part of my experience working with these missionaries in training is that my own young children caught a passion for missions that I believe they will hold onto the rest of their lives—perhaps having already received a calling since they often talk about going to the Nations. This did not happen because of a program or a video; it happened because two young people—whom I cannot even mention by name because they serve in such hostile countries—were so in love with Jesus and so burdened by the lost that they overflowed with excitement and enthusiasm about what it means to truly "go make disciples."

When we talk about the Essential Nutrient of Culture Shaping, we must realize that the reason why it is essential is because the Great Commission is essential in our Christian faith. And it begins as soon as kids say yes to their walk with Jesus—their journey as a missionary starts at that moment. Our ultimate objective here should be to bring up kids who have a heart not just for their friends at school, but also for the Nations. The question is, are we bringing up the next generation of both goers and senders?

Many of our missionaries today were called at a young age—some of them at church camp and many of them at Vacation Bible School! Both of these experiences are what we like to call "mountaintop" experiences, where we prepare for months to have an intense week of learning and growing and sharing the gospel. These are also great times to share about our call, as Christ followers, to tell the world about Him. I pray that you would expose the kids and families in your ministry to all kinds of opportunities to participate in missions, including church-wide mission initiatives. Sometimes, churches forget to include children in this important work.

For example, invite families to participate in a commissioning service to send off both short-term and long-term missionaries. When those "goers" return, they can come talk to the Kids Ministry about their time serving—with pictures and stories and interesting objects they bring back, exposing them to other cultures that need the gospel.

If you're smart, you'll lovingly recruit some of those missionaries who have the gift of evangelism to your Kids Ministry. After all, it's our children who are next in line to "go," and the "sending" can begin now!

Sending involves praying for missionaries before they even go, raising money to send the missionary, and continuing to pray while they are away. Kids can get involved in raising money. Your Kids Ministry can be a catalyst for raising funds by doing creative projects such as consignment sales, baked goods sales, car washes, and lemonade stands. You can involve families in these efforts and affect whole households by igniting a love for God's people all over the world.

My prayer is that this chapter would energize you to strengthen the missions emphasis in your Kids Ministry, an objective that would nourish the hearts and souls of so many young ones who have the capability of shaping the culture and becoming the next goers and senders.

Conclusion

Fan the Flame: Stay Faithful in Your Calling

I am sure of this, that He who started
a good work in you will carry it on to
completion until the day of Christ Jesus.
—Philippians 1:6

I want to close by revisiting the same question I asked in the introduction of this book. Why did you get into Kids Ministry? We all have our "how" stories, but really evaluate the *why*. We do this because at some point in our journey, we

117

felt the call to children's ministry. It may have been a surprise to you or it may have always been your plan. Regardless of the path, we are all here together.

My prayer is that this little book has given you a ministry philosophy that you and your team can champion together. You can use it to fan the flame of your own calling and those surrounding you. The three Essential Nutrients of Kids Ministry are meant to help you lead a healthy ministry—one that is truly nourished with a Kingdom Expanding vision and foundation, a Heart Transforming mind-set with the gospel at the center of all you do, and a Culture Shaping urgency for kids to illuminate the darkness and be the next generation of senders and goers.

Just like Spurgeon reminds us, we are called to "feed lambs" and we should stand ready to "cheer on those whose chief calling is to attend to the young ones." That, my friend, is you. You are the cheered, but you are also the cheerleader. Children's ministry is the most important and urgent work of the Church as we equip the next generation to take on the culture they are inheriting from us. It is time to energize the

Church with this message and lead the change it takes to build armies of volunteers, teachers, and leaders.

In order to fulfill this calling, it is important to remember to rest. Carve out the time necessary to Sabbath and find joy in the Lord by spending time with Him. If you neglect to do this, the Enemy will find a way to get you too busy and ultimately cause you to burn out. The stakes are too high and the need for ministry to children and their families is too urgent to risk your leadership being under attack. Rest in the Lord so that you will have the wind in your sails to give it your all.

More than anything, I pray that you would stay faithful in your calling to kids ministry, remembering that with spiritual leadership can also come suffering. I pray that you would continue to lead and disciple others, multiplying yourself as you continue to serve alongside those who are also called. I know that our God will be faithful to equip you and provide all you need to endure the race to the end.

Notes

1. Charles Spurgeon, *Come Ye Children* (Christian Heritage, 2003), 1.

2. Priscilla Shirer, *Breathe: Making Room for Sabbath* (Nashville, TN: LifeWay Press, 2014), 10.

3. J. Oswald Sanders, *Spiritual Leadership* (Chicago, IL: Moody Publishers, 2007), 18.

4. Daniel Darling, "Why You Can't Push Your Kids into the Kingdom," (September 28, 2015), ERLC.org.

5. See LifeWay.com/levelsofbiblicallearning.

6. *The Big Picture Interactive Bible Storybook* (Nashville, TN: B&H Publishing Group, 2013), 6.

7. *The Gospel Project for Kids*, LifeWay Kids (Nashville, TN).

8. *The Gospel: God's Plan for Me* (Nashville, TN: LifeWay Press, 2012) is a sixteen-page pamphlet that explains the gospel in kid-friendly language.

9. Russell Moore, *Onward: Engaging the Culture without Losing the Gospel* (Nashville, TN: B&H Publishing Group, 2015), 9.

10. International Mission Board, Kidsonmission.org

About the Author

Jana Magruder serves as the Director of Kids Ministry for LifeWay Christian Resources and brings a wealth of experience and passion for ministry, education, and publishing. A graduate of Baylor University, she has written award-winning curricula, both interactive and traditional in nature, for the state of Texas, IMAX films, and international authors, as well as churches and ministries. She is also the author of *Life Verse Creative Journal*, which she cowrote with her daughter, Morgan Grace, for girls of all ages. In addition to their daughter, Jana and her husband, Michael, have two boys and reside in Nashville, Tennessee.

Were you nourished by this book? Consider sharing it with others! Here are a few ideas:

- Grab copies for your volunteer team and read it with them utilizing the "Food for Thought" questions at the end of each chapter.
- Recommend the book to your Kids Ministry friends, your local KidMin networks, or others on your church staff.
- Mention the book in your social media or blogs using the hashtag #kidsministrythatnourishes.
- Go to facebook.com/JanaLMagruder, "like" the page, and engage in further Kids Ministry conversations.
- Tweet: "If you're interested in leading a healthy kids ministry I recommend reading #kidsministrythatnourishes by @jana_magruder."

Ways to connect with Jana Magruder:

Facebook: facebook.com/janalmagruder
Twitter: @jana_magruder
Instagram: @lifeverse
Blog and podcast: lifeway.com/kidsministry
Conference: etchconference.com

Discover Your Life Verse
with the
Life Verse Creative Journal Set

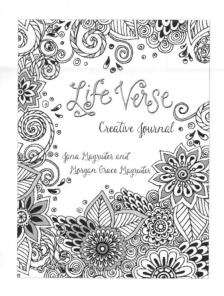

Choosing a life verse from Scripture is a powerful way to aim your steps toward God. This two-pack of beautiful journals will guide you to choose a life verse and to make it your own!

Available now!

B&H

Every WORD Matters™

BHPublishingGroup.com